In a Boston Night

poems

Sasenarine Persaud

We acknowledge the support of the Canada Council for the Arts for our publishing program and the Government of Ontario through the Ontario Arts Council.

Cover design by Heng Wee Tan
Author photograph: Tekil Persaud

Library and Archives Canada Cataloguing in Publication

Persaud, Sasenarine, 1958–
In a Boston night : poems / Sasenarine Persaud.

ISBN 978-1-894770-49-1

I. Title.

PS8581.E7495I6 2008 C811'.54 C2008-902899-6

Printed in Canada by Coach House Printing

TSAR Publications
P. O. Box 6996, Station A
Toronto, Ontario M5W 1X7
Canada

www.tsarbooks.com

In a Boston Night

CONTENTS

IN A BOSTON NIGHT

Sparkling in sideway eyes,
Florida lightening as bright
as a Krishna-blue bulb. To sit
near a dark wood stand casting
corner glances. Another day,
standing unexpected at my door—
do un-announce again, again—
spring bloom in late summer.
My unnecessary shirt a delay.

Will you wait? Flicking open hair
falls drenching us in threads
of black water sprays
(canoeing on the Little Manatee)
if you say—My wand is broken.
My book of seductions too dusty
for a recent SexHigh Graduate's touch,
kajal-streaked skin above calf boot
now on accelerator, now on clutch
distracted by the Hawaiian exploits:
aloha driving, aloha courtesy.

Who will be queen is queen. Rani.
Such a slice of cake we never saw,
mud pie, a prince extracting edible gems;
you licking his chocolate covered finger.
Across the Charles River, Harvard undergrads
singing from another car, to you, is new.

I was chanting a raga since that first look.
How long ago?—you will not hear,
ancient excuse, you do not know a raga!
Flick back your head, your hair. Small

Brad Pitt, lookalike, still is.
Who competes successfully with stars?
Or dreams of the Silver Screen. Just one
smile tomorrow enough. "I kid you not!"
My Floridian friend would say the opposite,
I want it now. I want it all, every time, and
if you will you will. If you must you must.

PARTING

I

No, I lie.
One long look today
is not enough.
First sight of toes I kiss.
If you say—"Yes!" Yes?
One more touch unenough.

II

Migraine and I not there
to hold your head. The
pain, this pain to chest.

III

When I last heard of Dover
Gloucester was blind
and walking off a cliff.
Or was that Lear? Poor
Cordelia hanged herself.
Or was that Lear?

WAITING NEAR THE CHARLES RIVER

I

The mobile's a bright blue screen.
Date and time, the server's name.
And mine. Strength of signal good.
Three bars—four black drinking-glass
bands. The message box icon
useless. The ringer silent. Your name
not appearing. Your voice unheard.

II

Two sides of the Charles—
Canada Geese cut diagonally
across to the boathouse—
we traversed that night,
back seat passenger.
The car filled this time.
I cannot touch head
or hair. I cannot touch
sheathed toes in boots.
I wait in the Charles, sail up,
for unforthcoming breath.

III

An hour has gone.
Still, the cardinal calls
in the dark.
Isn't he tired?
Will she not relent?
He says in the second anguished hour,
"I will share you with your lover."

IV

Mid-September: one sugar maple
Already turning a made-up cheek,
A deco-pink we used to know,
And love in Miami, in Toronto.

WHITE TIGER FROM THE TORONTO ZOO IN BOSTON

White pants, white shirt,
white shoes, white skin.
Once, in a maple-smothered cage,
I saw those rotating eyes—
look I cannot bear today
pleading: Take me home
take me home
take me home
on a violin-sitar raga sits
Yehudi Menuhin's India.

BACKING THE CHARLES

Reclining in a curved hollow on clipped grass
like newly weds, the writing cluster nibble
lips on the river singing an infection dissolving
in sprays. Taste this salt. We're going to change
the world, make a mark. Ivy laughed the wind
on the School of Social Work's red-brick wall.

One of two republicans was called a skinhead
in school—that wasn't hard to tell
another day wearing black leather—doc martens?
laced up like nooses above her ankles; the other
flicking straw hair, "Well I really, really don't care."

The democrats came in a tsunami,
twenty-foot waves thrashing a not-so-distant
Atlantic waistline: a wasteful war could buy
healthcare for the nation, that illiterate
cannot pronounce "nuclear", doesn't know
the name of the Canadian Prime Minister!

In the afterglow of a nugget we cannot see
beyond the horizon's grasp nothing matters—pixie—
not the fool's gold of alma maters, or of what
who has written, or published; not partners in Mehico
or experiences in near or distant September places
or a flushed silence no curiosity perforates . . .

But I will tell you in private, in the presence
of those famous words, the essence of fall
petals, ivy climbing for that indigo illusion
and brass-white blossoms drifting into the South
End Southie—Aye, mih friend, it is that time O'time.

Maybe she will visit Glasgow. A nano-drop of blood
falls on the grass as we dust off in the dusk.

FIRST STORMS

I

It rained this morning
on red eyes Boston's
first thunder—you think
Ophelia's reached New England
and Toronto's come south
of the border. We stretch for
a raindrop's water touch
pave and runnels to ocean.

II

Should I come down this morning,
love, and enter another storm?
Indra-streaks and Thor-claps,
but I will miss your learning—
if I remain, will I miss that longing
smile on every sheltered face?
Stay wind, stay water from our clothes
though if these are wet undress undress.
Who will lend a slicker? To come expecting
winter, instead this tropical water. So,
should I come down this morning,
love, and revel in a Boston storm?

III

And not quite as quickly
it has come and gone.

IV

This chipped brown desk
with a hundred scars and nicks
matched by the battered chiffonier's
red-brown good looks: stains
hiding the steady hands of an
anonymous craftsman's etchings
of rose blossoms and a leather oval
will be just as they are now
when I first walked in this room
shielding secrets, leaning on ghosts
of other lives, and now our own.

MORNING AFTER

Boil of food-court chatter.
A sparrow making sorties.
Fingers spilling crumbs
and stale bitter coffee.

UNPLANNED

Snow clutched in the V's sprawling
fling of careless limbs after sex—
who did not employ a contraceptive,
or a rubber, academic now. Walking
along an ocean's edge of doubt will drive
us to the sofa first, arguing like lovers,
and when we least expect, a flurry of
soft-packed skin. We disengage before,
spattering your victory on a windscreen
destined for the wiper blades in five seconds
who will, or not, say—no, please, no babies.

STREET FAIR: BROOKLINE 300

They are dismantling the tents in the dusk.
The steel poleframes clanging as they fall
to the ground. We are still sitting on the tarmac
under a few leaves yellowing in the September sun
a folk artist singing, "This land is my land"
and then, "Where have all the flowers gone—gone
for graveyards everyone." You are not supposed
to cry for strangers, young men who have come back
from the desert draped in red white and blue,
but you do, quietly. The girl with the leashed gray-black
cat—looking, like you, for a pickup—dancing (is she
drunk?) like the Odissi and Kuchipudi dancers
we just saw, accompanied by the Indian flautist (a doctor),
the Indian veena player (another doctor), the mridangam player
(a scientist). For thirty minutes we are artists giving India
to the world for free—and again at MIT in two months.
It is all we have left. You have misnamed our numbers
calling them *Arabic Numerals;* the windows operating
system, not Bill Gates, an Indian scientist developed.
You have taken our yoga, renaming it in the *New York
Times* today, Christian Yoga and now Jewish Yoga
right here in Boston we must ask The Master, Iyenger,
what else can we give you Brookline?
What else can we give you World?

BIRD

The black-capped chickadee said:
I'm in a monogamous relationship
I live in Puritan New England
I never heard of the *Gitanjali* or Mormons.

MOURNING

A mother lost
is a mother waiting
to be found. Grief
is not a migraine
it is a whole life.

LUNCH

The mountain-wheeled cycle locked to a campus lamppost
Asks another: where is your studious rider?
What hands held your handlebar grips?
What legs massaged your saddle? One answered,
do not speculate except if you mean to be a philosopher.
In the leaf-spotted quadrangle, a man pushes a stroller
with the pride of a first time father. There is no mother now.
In the leaf-splattered courtyard, a woman delves into her bag,
lines up a wax paper-wrapped sandwich, yogurt, a large red
apple
and we are as hungry as we were in Miami, in Toronto.

READING STEINBECK IN PUBLIC

Do not chew in class.
Nobody said, do not consume
Grapes in public lest juice
trickle down your face:
a man at a truck stop heading to California
wants ten cents worth of a fifteen-cent loaf;
and Mae making a nickel-a-piece candy
worth two for a penny for a pair of
farm siblings. Dustbowl fiction
sprinkling such particles of heart, the spirit
of a people soaring on a biscuit-crisp
morning ideal for rowers on the Charles.

Beware echoes. Do not eat grapes in public
lest the clear juice stain your eyes
and the girl with the red toes
at the table nearby gets up abruptly—
afraid to see you cry.

AUDIENCE: WALCOTT IN BOSTON

Looking up, did you see the bottom
of a Caribbean blue krial
changing shape in the wind, bearing
the static particles' quarrels with history:
Language producing a lightening Raghu arrow

or the thunder of dholaks during Ramlila,
the story of the *Ramayana* re-enacted
on the plains of Caroni? An assistant
whispering. We waited. You looking over
History's spectacles—reading the fine prints

of contracts, or revising Couva's sadhu
can't wait, won't wait, fed on Gita
will traipse Indian mountains
or Trinidad's, Brookline's byways leading
to Commonwealth Ave—nodding green eyes
over the rims of New England provincials.

A Canadian journalist exposing her heart's
burden in the *Globe and Mail* immediately after
The Announcement: you made a pass in a hotel
room, cursed out white people, brought up the bile
of slavery on being rebuffed. Man to West
Indian man wanting to meet our greatest

living poet cannot recall that meeting
in Toronto—not so speckled headed then,
or like the painting on a cover of Conrad's
Secret Agent, not impressionistic, not reposing
on a couch with a carving knife in your chest.

Fiction converging with fictitious poetry's
metre and rhythm and feet, an instructor's:
don't say what isn't, say what is
isn't Hindu. Cocktail acquaintance
with the *Upanishads*: "Not by light
is It grasped, not even by speech
not by any other sense organ, not by . . ."

No, you did not brush us off in Toronto.
The faraway stare was settled on Homer,
the fiction of an island Hector battling Achilles,
Stockholm's Helen germinating Paris' seed
or Boston's. Where did you compose
Your fine lie? BU paying as you read

your famous V.S. Nightfall poem, reciting
in one West Indian dialect few in the auditorium
understand Caribbean-speak a rebellion like,
not (an Indian will speak in negatives) a Boston
Tea Party, but a rum-and-coconut-water party's
ingredients from an Indian cultivar of grass,

even coconuts came from somewhere east,
not native to those islands you will battle
over. V.S. truer to ancestral nothingness
than all our metaphoric pyrotechnics'
search for the original and new, a folk song

"Sancho lick he lover pun deh dam
And deh gyal a'halla murder
Bip bap police a'come
and deh gyal a'halla murder . . ."

Almost all your work still in the Queen's
King's English: at least you knew changing

colour to color and harbour to harbor,
honour to honor didn't make a new language.
A New York publisher understanding. Galassi
sounds Italian. A Florida rain pounding

the red brick patio's puddles outside
like bullets, a rain that worried Plunkett
and the pig-minder's wife, Maud. Comm Ave
is damp and cold and I didn't have to explain
how those graduate playwrights hated
your making one woman weep, almost,
with a question: "How Jewish is Jewish?

How Jewish are you?" We are roving
over the West Indian universe, coffee
in a restaurant reflecting creek-coloured
pupils, yet I ask that question you asked
knowing she would shut off that standpipe
offer and we would go our ways—
to New York to Florida. Not suddenly,
cat each other a little longer, with grace
to India to Israel—skin a Japanese silk

in the stores of Jackson Heights, Queens
not far from her childhood enclave
where another West Indian, Khan,
invited us to a dinner he sculpted from ancestry:
a dozen dishes from India his Jewish partner
of a decade never knew—we licked fingers.

Jew and Moslem cohabiting were neither
Chosen nor Islamist; Hindu guests not Hindu
having come from that same soil: words
and after-dinner stories; unforgotten incidents
igniting like lightening: Who Derek? At a conference

on Caribbean Literature, right here in Brooklyn,
some years ago, he said to me—only Indian
participant—"Ismith, what you coolies doing here?
This is black people thing, you know . . ."

And so if in your Omeros islands there are blacks
and whites only, we understand in a great epic
a great living poet cannot be burdened
with being politically correct, with
reproducing a microcosm of his society.

Such quotas are required only of minor poets
and minor writers: the *Times* review of *Jumbie Bird*
declaring that if Mr Khan thinks this Indian only
fiction is Trinidad, he must be mistaken.
Succumbing to the critics, he was never to create
as well on anyone on anything Indian until then—

a dozen Indian dishes none of the women present
could replicate. It is raining. Plunkett rain.
Maud rain. Thunder ripping the silence,
flashes like ghost roots breaking the dark masonry
and all this is gone in a green glance over lens

for reading fine print, for revising "The Sadhu
of Couva" or *In a Green Night*. Yesterday,
there was sun at the party: kids splashing
in the "blue pools of paradise"—you can lick
it, our host said, "chatey" if you like. British/American
wives and children not understanding the laughter

host adding: we would wipe the saucepans
clean with roti; not your fancy metropolitan
saucepan, a West Indian's—five pound tin

of ghi or butter or skimmed milk converted
to a blackened pot for cooking sauces

of an hundred delights—a saucepan Hector
and Achilles would battle over. Where are the Indians
of St. Lucia? There are Indians there, are there not?
My father always asking: Have you done your homework?
The shipwrecked Indian almonds you will highlight

in Sweden. A grace only great poets posses
at the same time as such a curiosity makes
a woman playwright cry and her colleagues not
like you. "You from Trinidad?" suddenly,
the pleasantries over. Achilles was slain by Paris
the archer. We forget this in the books,
in the rigmarole of the wooden horse. "No."

My grandparents would have preferred
Raghu-Rama, celestial bowman. Achilles knew
the gods were never wrong. He was wrong
and then he was right. Even epic heroes die—
I have lunch with my daughter—in Boston
in a cold monsoon fall, in an olive three-piece . . .

And you could audit any one of my poetry lectures.
Forget the requirements—being West Indian . . .

You remember Rohan Kanhai's backside-on-the-pitch
hook to the boundary, cricket's tiger cleaving
in an-almost-winter reading of BU faculty,
the auditorium overflowing. Speech of the islands
as tricky as a spinner's wicket is English. It was
just one stanza, but man, Nightfall haunts us all—still.

IN THE EYES OF CONQUISTADORS

Because we will never remove a dark smudge
from your calf again, or ride in front
up a steep incline, or listen to a drunken boy
singing a song in Cambridge, "Roll up
skirt, peel off panty, make love in a car."
Pinsky's party not far away—nor Hawaii.

But we are leaping like Hanuman, as leaping is
necessary to set fire to Ravan's capital
in your dark eyes, if we stay we get burnt—
where there is fire, is there a fireman
waiting to attempt a rescue? You are gone
in the smoke of my childhood capital burning

in the smoke of conquistadors' swords
glinting in a tropical sunlight, the pink river
of natives' blood—if you are native to America
so am I—only south south and way more south
where bats rattle their thousand wings like
fields of chattering grasshoppers and the dusk

drops its dark curtain suddenly
and stars come out like the teeth of mice
nibbling at the blanket around your heart
and you are young again and long after
bringing gypsy eyes, India-smooth skin;
a princess who came from China

is Vikramaditya's not yours not yours
not yours because we will never make love
on a tropical hardwood floor
sit on a warm seawall as the sun settles in the dust
of the land on the ocean, or on an Easter morning
reading a web of kites glorify our eyes

too close together like strings and kite tails
tangling as our legs will never
twine. And the tall lighthouse sinking
two inches, or six, each year, while ships pass
into the Demerara River or out to the ocean—
India too far for who will not have wet kisses

or dry, because I will never touch your heart
again, or your foot, with the wild fire of youth
and the passion of a six o'clock beetle
singing to the whole of an overgrown village
and my city of desires you will never know.

"HALF A LIFE"

It rained all that day and the day after
and we are driving through the mountains
of Connecticut uncertain of a new life;
and were you, whom I didn't know
yet, whom I may have passed
on a stretch of the Massachusetts Turnpike

August 29 or 30 a blurred rainscreen
can never be for you—
JFK Airport, Costco, Van Wyck, the Belt
Parkway—New York we leave behind
nothing to a mother who has left
whom you do not know you miss

at seven and ma gone. Nothing I can tell
you do not know: how for years
I cried when no one looked, and even
when they did and even now; you lose
a mother and lose and gain half a life.

ISLAND

On a green Atlantic as rough as pine boxboards
used to make pallets and later knocked down to make
rooms (if you rub your fingers carelessly splinters
thinner than hair), the boats of the leisured catch
the sly wind, cutting a line across the Vineyard ferry.

On the stelling, we left blue-uniformed men
tending German dogs near the crowded gangway.
Here is the playground of the wealthy, or an ageing
Irish democrat, summer retreat of The Commander, but
for you, a childhood: *I want to show this carousel.*

You fling the brass rings around the pole to win a free ride.
You sit in this community shed and sing gospels—the whole
town. You listen to the old-timers dropping in all day to speak
with mom: all the black families, that is, and their cousins.
You work summers in a store still owned by the same family.

Gingerbread houses untouched since the Civil War: wood
decorated the colors of flowers speckling front yards
and side yards and the crowd of souvenir hunters in the
town centre. *This is the bandstand where of a Saturday*
the orchestra played classical music—exactly like that one

of your British childhood. Today is not about me.
Look, the Canada geese have taken over now, and their thick
curly droppings—careful where you place your feet. That
is Norton's, the antivirus man's house. Burnt down, rebuilt
exactly—well, with insulation. Nobody stays in the winter

or past October. Look, clapboard houses. I grew up in one
all year round. We are talking now, over tea, of other
times when there were proposals and lovers: *And*

as you know, the later lies. He was two, three-timing
me. But it's got to go when I get back. Clouds flare their

underwear at the sinking sun like the little girls we left behind:
cousins, a sister. We must take our leave. Compressing a history,
a lifetime in a single afternoon is an art I have yet to learn. And
you can tell as we say farewell at the stagnant ferry line. *Call*
me now and then, come back. See you in Florida. Goodbye
to roundabouts, the drive back to a Boston night,
stars in our eyes.

CARIBBEAN FALL

Red sumacs burning eyes
under the Boston University Bridge,
we need glasses
to see toes in imitation fur;
discussing Jamaican Creole
in books, *Summer Lightning*,
black-brown hair I can't remember—
what is the flavour of the day?—
a strand dislodged from the bun,
hot cross bun on Good Friday
or Good Thursday or Saturday?
exposing a road up the nape—
what we need is coffee
to thaw fingers, wag our tongues
on Harris like Senior, or Naipaul
on Selvon. We need glasses
to see what we've left behind,
a shot of optimism, as we thread
cascading hickory-gold leaves.

BOSTON FALL

You creep stealthily up to one window
while I am looking down another
for a past we cannot leave behind.
You shed your apparel in ones and threes and tens,
a patch of yellow on the maple, rust-red
on an oak. When did the grass become straw
and the blue jays arrive in droves
caterwauling: screams like a cartwheel's
spokes from all around? After six years, or ten,
you finally arrive at my desolate
window like a bridegroom's party
and I am still empty.

ANOTHER MORNING AFTER

Rain trickling down the rails in the night
tapping on the windowsill like a quiet
dholak and a sitar of soft moans.
The morning a Krishna-coloured dusk
in which the golden flecks on clouds
is bested by the drip of maple leaves
on the wet boarding-house tarmac next door
all the green and black vehicles speckled
and decorated like just-married cars
silent after the wedding—husbands
and wives having taken to bridal suites.
We wait again for the creaking of beds.

RED SUMACS

Burn my eyes
take Boston chill
away from fingers.
I may write a line
or two, a fiction
for a seminar,
a scholarly paper's
lies on a novel.

Heat my eyes
take cold
away from throat.
I may send a raga
to your paper lips,
lemongrass tea
eyes we haven't
tasted in a *janam*

—what is that?—the
glossary's a hindrance
the professor makes a
circle with thumb
and finger, sticks
another in and out;
this, a story needs
to show. Back to
you I say
burn my eyes
burn my throat
burn my heart
burn every part
every ounce of art.

CREATIVE WRITING

One said: Her backflip in the creek
seems improbable. How could a
whirlpool form, pull at him
and not her? Your language is weird
your prepositions an adventure.
Do you really want Americans (whites?
US passports do not make the Indians
of Liberty Avenue, or Jackson Heights,
Queens—40 years here—Americans?)
to read your book! And don't say we *stole*
your vegetarianism, your yoga, your numbers
and misname them Arabic Numerals. And
what foreign language your characters speak!
You use too many Indian words.
Who has time for glossaries? Don't tell us
about politics, or the polluting factories of NJ
or a white woman, sour from last night's sex,
who doesn't bathe on winter mornings.

Revision: we must only give you love, or the evils
of Hinduism. We do not know the beggars—as organized
as in Dickens' London—or the Mumbai roadside
shitters. We can always give you *Gandhi*, the movie,
pretend we were not born in the New World, that we are
Indian. But how to write a bastard self? That you
could not teach in a thousand *janams*. What?

REVISION, WORLD WAR II

All deaths not equal,
he said gloomily:
Russians lost 20 million
in WW II—Jews 6–7 million,
who ever hear about Russian dead?
I never knew until now
that gypsies went to the ovens too:
"the cockroaches of Europe."

WALKING DOWNHILL

New brownstones stand like flamingoes
on the backside of Summit Hill,
their long-legged decks facing north.
What views in summer, and what barbeques
and gathering of friends. Leaves flutter down
yellow and brown, crisp paper underfoot.

In the Indian summer dusk, you rake vigorously
scraping up bottom layers sticking to the asphalt,
tights following the season of buttock seam under
back to front. It will be the same next year; we will be
elsewhere, following that curve of spring into fall.

NOVEMBER OAKS ON THE DRIVE TO PLYMOUTH ROCK

Russet on a fleece blanket in a pioneer village
not quite north of Toronto. Brown on a woolen jersey,
on a frayed bedstead on the thighs of Mount Tremblant
earth-orange. The undersides of the last holdouts
are the marks of beard-pummeled cheeks in a southern
heat will tell our friends tomorrow—or tonight—
why did you not give a little cry, my love, or
raise my chin away with your whisper-finger touch?

LUNATIC SPEAKING TO MAPLES & SUMACS ON A WET FALL DAY

Sugar gone from your leaves
the flame from your tongues
dribbling to the ground
like a kite let go by Brahmin fliers.

You can't mock my grammar
and my Caribbean usage till spring.
You can't laugh my molasses rhythm
and my tiger-jumping imagery

from Boston to Calcutta
Demerara to Toronto.

Your limbs sticking the sky are brambles
black as scalded tongues
bare as cobwebs shrouded with dust,

spittle leaking down the lips of your cunt
like—name-dropping—Jimmy's Naipaul.

XVI: THE FLAME OF SHIVA—A PHALLUS?

I honour the Romans
using their numerals
you the Vikings
and Eric the Red
bringing love of god
and man and child
in the days before
corner-store contraception.

Ah, I am mistaken. We honour, instead,
(knowing my metahistory)
that flame of Shiva's: a faint memory
of mommy offering honeyed milk
at dawn and dusk, when kiskadees sing
and bats flap their wings like tracers,
to a Shiva lingam encircled by a yoni.

THANKSGIVING

For Dedham Rock cemented
somewhere in the middle of that last break-up:
ten years. A schoolboy's promise
under the spittle of a fountain outside
the Ontario Science Centre. Tasting
a cousin's ganja and a blooded organ
flushed like fall dogwoods in a sheltered yard,
last pepper leaves before tomorrow's flurries:
turmeric corn, lime peas, flaky roti, curried Yukon,
Basmati—she went to London—rice, baked turkey—
enough, enough, you ass, shut down the computer.
We're saying grace for November flower,
Indian hawthorn's tiny fruit: red. The rock one third
original size; recollection of pubic lips saltier
than Atlantic sprinkles—grace, please, grace—sweet.

"A FEATHER ON THE BREATH OF GOD"

(*JH reading from* Mrs Kimble)

Spread a butterfly's wings
in front your lips,
touching ceiling and floor—
not a fleck of insect powder
dislodged, *Mrs Kimble Mrs Kimble.*
Monarch dust on your hair
art-deco orange, pixie on our ears,
Mrs Kimble Mrs Kimble . . .
I can wait all day outside your door.

BOSTON UNIVERSITY BRIDGE

For walks on the promenade we will never take
across brown steel girders backing Beacon Hill
to stop midway and contemplate the Charles
like Wordsworth—or was that Keats—looking on
a lover, not capital of Empire—this is my London
and my Thames up which the Koh-i-Noor glitters.
We are putting out in a *ballyhoo—The Oxford*
Dictionary of Caribbean English Usage—

For a Polish heart of darkness or an Indian
bend in the river, sail me through ancestors
and the green hearts of Rome, a piling in Venice
floating down the Demerara to a mill
on the east shore processing turmeric poles,
a splint in our eyes, sawdust, gazing up
in the chapel: Michelangelo Michelangelo
or Jackie Hunter done Jackie Hunter done (plagiarist!)
This flavor of desire's a match flare ending fall.

WINTER BURGLAR

Before nightfall, your powder wraps
every shrub and lower branch
with Niagara froth. This winter's just
begun. The dark uppers of swinging
maples planted in another century's
infancy are the last holdouts.
Your leotards dust window glass.
We cannot see our yard as you swirl
in and take Patanjali to copyright.
We are flipping to the weather channel:
a winter storm. *These are the facts*, you say.
So far this year, 150 patents were issued
for yoga postures in the West—134 in old USA.

No, we do not dislike your devildust, sticky
and cold—aren't they pretty—ah, these glasses
you prescribed, eggshell thin, photo-grained,
scratch-coated: the best. I see sharply. Yoga
lens made in America. What, we can't say
"yoga"? You're filing a patent for this too?
Like our bitter *neem* you patented
and lost in the World Court in The Hague.
These are the facts, you say, *You must now pay*
to use your ancient name—like it or yoga it.

A FABLE: WAITING FOR THE SNOW TO THAW

Pull the blinds. Why? *Shut out the glare.*
It's not as bad as sun on white sands
among rainforest; sands so crystalline
the Chinese—Mao extending his Cultural
Revolution to El Dorado to redden the world—
built a massive glass factory. *In the bush?*
Yes, surrounded by tall never-harvested trees.
What kinds of trees? O, just trees. All trees are trees.
We didn't define every shrub and leaf and plant:
oak or beech, or sumac, ash, maple, holly or molly.
Okay, okay: mora, sliverballi, wallaba, kabakalli. . .

The bottles came with tumours in their necks,
vases with sores on their shins. They worked that out.
A factory like a square palace in the forest.
How does a tiny country consume all those bottles
and drinking glasses and figurines and vases? Who
needed vases anyway? We loved our flowers on plants,
a year-round bloom surrounding our houses—except
the blacks grew nothing in their yards. *What a
racist thing to say!* True. There were exceptions.

But if you drove along that "Wild Coast of South America"
you knew Indian village: painted houses, rainbow of blooms;
from black village: bare yards, or overgrown, brown homes,
men loitering around the village shop . . . *What a racist thing
to say!* O, we said it all; "Coolie wata-rice pork and spice,"
"Blackman sala, bandar sala," "Putagee bumba,
fart cucumber," "Ching-Leung-Too can't open he eye"
"White man bakra, goat sit high." *You guys were so racist!*
So we were, indeed, like Dixie and Yankee and
east and west and KKK, wop, buck, and honkey.

What happened to the glass factory? Erratic electricity.
Mao died. The Cultural Revolution died. Our Kabaka
died. It rusted. The heat was too much. The vines
encroached. Workers stole parts. It was too far
from the city. The Chinese embassy cut back on its
subsidies and staff Mercedes—socialists you know,
communists you see. I must ask my distant relatives:
a red elephant or a rusting one? So open the curtains. Let
the glare blind these voices in our heads; trample memory.

Why are we waiting? For the snow to thaw, for
the day to warm up so the car can come out,
so we can make snowballs like kids and fling
our pasts at each other, and laugh and look
at your cheeks and nose glow red like fairy lights
and come back, wined on the cold, cuddle on the couch,
and you can examine my brown-bag skin for your paper
and I your nipples—like purple sea grapes—for a poem.

HER DANCING ON LEAVES: RE-READING *PALACE OF THE PEACOCK*

We sat, not a desk apart,
side by side in a lecture, travelling through
the savannah's tall grass. Donne on
a white horse in a canter—"A shot rang out."
He was dead, we thought, captain of a surly crew
on a Guyana river approaching the rapids.
I was born there, I shout, unable to hold it longer.
Where? On the river? Near the beautiful Mariella?

Barefoot, I saw her once, a baby on her back.
The forest leaves six inches thick on the trail.
We passed her slowly on the truck. Someone
waved. She blinked and smiled. *Taking food*
for her husband at the logging site. Her body firm,
her skin buff copper in the sun-starved quiet
we disturbed. The Bedford's hum in low gear
could not drown her dancing on leaves; a rattle, a drum—

or later still as we neared the camp,
the cries *Timber! Timber!* We cut the engine.
After a hundred years, her husband felled
the tallest greenheart in the stand, the best.
We crowded around, coastlanders, to glimpse
his massive trunk. The chatter resumed.
Chainsaws screamed. Business concluded, we left
the noise and the brittle quiet. That was when we saw
the butterflies. One, two, following us like dolphins.

On a forest trail, there's only one way the Bedford
could go—as slow as a Sunday afternoon stroll
on the Promenade near the bandstand looking
to England across the Atlantic. Blue butterflies' wings

like tennis rackets driving, with topspin, escaped straws
of sunlight through the umbrella of leaves overhead,
thinking, her son reading this might say, *I was born there!*

Sparkling cobalt wings alight on the green leaves
in your aquamarine eyes. Her bare toes hidden
in the socks of russet twigs we finally see in yours
hoisted on the chair in front. I see her every time
I see that forest, that forest every time I see your eyes.
Donne is dead. We have scaled the cliff face. Someone,
the boy, Carroll, is playing a human femur flute

and the thick snow outside makes it look like
Christmas—the holidays. After the last lecture, I close
the book, look around, chat with Professor Schomburgh.
There's nobody as I descend the stairs in the rock. Pausing
to zip my coat, you appear like an Amerindian walking
in the bush, the baby on your back haversacked books,
unwrapping the scarf to say you're going home.
I knot the silk around my throat, look to the nearest
door. I wish you luck for your finals, and your stay in Rome.

In your eyes are the merging of the green and blue
of my exile. You take the long corridor slowly—
I the closest door. An exile is always lonely, I would
call after your back, we tend to look behind once
in a while. I head outside instead, the Boston snow
like white sand on the edges of a tropical forest—
I went there once, enchanted. I loved—was born there—
a shout rang out. We died and yet we lived and lived again.

CHRISTMAS

White webs in winter are difficult to see
on the garage ceiling—four months worth
looking like frail cotton on Gandhi's handloom.
We vacuum the spiders too, survey the fall's
accumulation of *senna* spots running lazily
down the outer concrete walls. The millet border
paint has grown thicker. We stir cautiously; blot
the stains (until next year) dancing at the edges
of the rust harvest. Vehicles arrive and squeeze
every inch of driveways. Brushes and fingers
washed; the Florida sun rubbing our heads
like Granny's hand as she poured fresh coconut oil
in our hair: an ancient ayurvedic practice—
for little boys whose mother has passed?
"Dead" is an archaic word.

Might we have had streamers from window to ledge, or
scents of an overfilled oven working overtime for Old Year's
mingling with that of sulphur from the hammered rolls
of red caps curling out of heavy navy colts, or the starbursts
of red squib paper lining the waxed floor. Who jumped
when the hammer came down on crisp almond nut shells?
Or Granny pouring frothy ginger beer or sweet rice
wine to go with the tropical fruit cake, her cat arching its
back against your calf under the laden table—kicking
puss away before granny returns with the mug—I don't know,
really. I don't know—if your mother were here . . .

It's too windy for badminton, Daddy! Cricket?
Yes, please! You spin the ball in your wrist, like this.
You angle your bat down, so the ball sweeps the ground,
like this. You move your feet as you move your bat, like
this—the lemon flannel ball bouncing down the driveway
like an Afro-Guyanese flautist in the year-end masquerade.

I listen for a carol from that childhood mine, "Silent Night,
Holy Night . . ." or "I saw Three Ships Come Sailing in . . ."
These new hurricane-wary bungalows can swallow a shout. I
hear "Jingle Bells" on last night's violin-dholak-sitar medley.
Time for dinner! We file in like cricketers; later, finishing last
week's chess game, after Andy Rooney, a cup of hand-picked
Hill Tea and Ravi Shanker's Chants for a Beatle:
Guru Brahma Guru Vishnu, Guru Dev Maheshwara . . .

NO PROMISES FOR THE NEW YEAR

Sunlight wanders over the fence
and house tops like those stealthy lover's
touches we denied in Brookline.
It is all we can offer from New Tampa:
the proximity of the number one US beach
for 2005, Blue Ribbon sand smooth as your skin,
kids fishing for butterfly shells yesterday.

We have changed the car's oil, checked
her fluids, blackened our fingers
in her service. What would you have us do?
Dye our hair? Lose our ties to the Sunshine State?
Winterize the old vehicle. It works well yet,
as the Jamaican writer would say,
its hood rises as straight as a coconut tree

and we still have our Kali's tongue
(lust controlled) and your fabled quiet Indian.

GOODBYE TO THE HOLIDAYS

That first night, as the children prattled like parrots,
glad to have us back after a fall absence,
and our eyes kissed over their heads—we couldn't
wait for their bedtimes—I was delighted to be home.

Sounds of thorn gift-wrapping, violins and voices
merging with the school's Christmas chorus, returning
carols from our childhoods. Fruitcake, someone whispers.
We both hear it. You look around. She is not here.

Not only children move on in your absence.
Between visits and visitors, we arrive at that place
we had stopped. Unholy silences. Blinding glares.
Those canines that escape lips—flung over children's heads—

we'd promised to save for the master bedroom.
We could never become our parents,
could we? My father's rum, and since I do not drink,
my mother's poison, or your parents'—of whom I promised

never to speak or write—one promise I can still keep.
I skip the divorce notices, bypass the stories of the stars'
lovers in the *Sunday Times*, pack my bags, give a perfunctory
hug, scratch my list of tender things I did not do. Next time.

STONE ON MY HEAD

Burn this shell of tea-stained teeth
and graying hair, when consciousness
takes flight from body—if you can.
Scatter my ashes in the clucking Atlantic

as we did your grandfather's and mine.
And if by chance it is in some remote place
or wayward village, and I am coffined
like my mother, shoved in a tomb

surrounded by palms, do not pelt me with earth;
someone placing a wet clump in my tiny hand,
women chanting strange songs from a holy land,
and when no one looked letting the dirt fall at my foot.

Long after, when my uncle came from his jaunt
deep in the South American bush he placed the soil
I dropped, and a stone, on her grave—why, why,
I cried. If you will, plant a tree for flower

or fruit or shade, for bird, for beast, for bat.
But do not place a stone on my head
at any time, please do not place a stone on my head

LETTER FROM THE BLUE

You said (and a poet is exact)
what we had
and have
and will again
shall always be unique

maple seeds in pods
stored in a gray envelope
a smile recalling a smile
are things you keep close—
like declining parents

I tend wounded brass
that grows dull with age
and non-usage; an eastern bell
dongs Shiva's dance
of dissolution of an age
or period; it is always
the end of something

SNOWBANKS

Papercrisp banks of New England
snow as smooth as the first night thighs
of someone you used to know. Do not
mourn for a sun eclipsed by the flakes
hitting your cape. A proud pine branch
ridden by accumulation bends and touches
the pave in front, and behind as you pass.

No, no, stand up, you want to shout
I am no samurai. You turn a corner
onto the main street sidewalk
slipping once, twice in the fresh boot prints.
Stepping to the side, there is better traction.
You learn: It is easiest to walk on un-trodden snow.

SNOW FALLS ON ITSELF: WONDERFUL "K"

One said, I was born in Brookline
spent a month here, then went back
to the Holy Land. Small face spots
like moles, wanting to taste
honey brown eyes and Palestine milk.

Another looked a picture of Elizabeth I . . .
You need to be more accurate!
Well, a royal portrait: a thin curvature
of nose, a long arching forehead—
no, it was Isabella looking down

on Columbus. What was his name before
conversion? In Boston, holy Brookline
whispers he was a Jew. She said, and
we had to lean forward, I know Hindi
and Sanskrit, too. I have forgotten all

the others: Emma with a lisp and protruding
underlip; Lonie's head Yul Bryner's; Tess
the landlord's daughter—all except, she
said, *I am wonderful, wonderful Kate!*
Jumping like a Cossack, kicking heels.
I'd miss my chance, everyone gone

before I wrapped my scarf, the zipper
of the unkind coat slipping. Outside
beyond the chapel and the Charles River
a milk mist thickens and snow falls on itself.

THE LIGHTHOUSE

Thorns pricking through trousers
did not stick your fingers
laughing a removal: "from childhood"

circling the white base, tapering
to kohl eyelash designs, windows knocked out
by flames or firemen outing a lightning strike

walking around on sand
and the oldest guide in South—all
Florida—a baby calling as we turn away

GENESIS 3:17

If you had touched that soil of South America
At the edge of the forest, dark brown
And loose as grains. If you had seen
Its children: four feet long-bean, cassava
Longer than an arm and thicker than a thigh
Or tasted of a bucketful of spice mangoes
Sweeter than sex, you would know
This earth is our mother and our father.
And you would not curse it sand and rock
Or chase a man and his rib—an oasis
The arc of your knowledge—spaceman.

ARTANA GALLERY

A blue and white fleur-de-lis
flagging the mist and rain of a Boston night.
We thought this was an exhibition of art
is artifice, older women with long noses.

You need a cap? Needles? Knitting yarn?
I would be a prime candidate for the falling
blade. I unwrap my neck and the silk
gifted from Toronto. "I like your scarf!"

Indeed. In Brookline's Booksmith
last night, you fingered a tome of the Seven Years'
War—how Britain won and sowed the seeds
of its greatest loss south of the St Lawrence

Wolfe lay dying on the cover
of the Plains of Abraham: that struck our eyes
you see, blue and white forever bon jour bon jour
bon jour, compliments of the Quebec Delegation

French wine French cheese, perhaps,
the crackers too. The paintings now: garish.
That is too easy—paint like La Bamba, Aztec

macaw colours, except the nude sitting
one limb open, the fruit in her Genesis garden
shaded black. You know the painter
is a woman, not even that: Québecois.

In February, all the trees except conifers
are plucked. We might have gone out,
returned with a maple leaf from Bunker Hill
to carry our war everywhere. Or apple blossoms

of Morningside (east of Toronto) our hearts
outside a Boston night; land which gave love
new life—O Canada, what can I give you tonight?

GREEN LINE, BOSTON

Street car slowly passing a familiar face.
What are you doing on the opposite platform
wearing a monkey-blue peacock dress,
a frock over new faded jeans? You are
supposed to be gone. You are searching
the night for the perfect imagery. You are
that which we see, cannot get, cannot be.

INVERTING THE SUN

In a great city—
they made the declaration
from a balcony (in a house) here—
it is easy to transpose
the sign of a red sun
on a blue bag: the woman
in white coat, in black
heeled ankle boots, pointed,
running for the bus. It is
February—20°F and Surya
dances over the tops of buildings
to the south of Comm Ave;
get used to it, Bostonians abbreviate
everything, and it is easy
to transpose the sign of a blue sun
on a red bag on the shoulder
of a running woman in the early morning

BLUE-STRIPED DRESS

Girl in a blue-striped dress
on an unpaved road: tiny stones
protruding from the gravel
at your brown-shoed feet.
Girl turning against the wind
holding hair in place
the hem of a dress in a breeze
going across the canal—we almost
drowned there—twenty years
or twenty thousand, girl in a blue
striped photograph, left behind, lost.

BOSTON CHEEK

Bundled up, three layers, not counting underwear.
Where have all the open-toes gone, milk
flavoured necks, New England—how do you
say that Southie—I thumb my nose at you sir,
the wind. I crack my goose to let in air
loosen the sheep around my throat. Hood up
(not in Jamaican creole) you pass bowed into
the west wind: red face, red face, red face
is that what they call natives then? Ha,
I'm headed east. Apples bloom in February
below your eyes, gulab jamuns soaked in red wine.

IN A CITY THAT LOVES TO HATE REDCOATS

Upside down mermaid tails,
turrets tiled like fish scales
and casement windows, frosted.
Did I hear you say Victorian Era?
Houses mimicking British castles.
In this city of The Declaration
of Independence, mini-coopers, pea cars
of England owned by Germans (old
royal cousins and enemies, too) dart in
and out of parking spaces like mice.

SPRINGS: TORONTO-BOSTON

Suddenly, the naked limbs stirred
from their cold sleep shooting
tiny shards in all directions:
shrapnel? No, Bostonians don't use
such things! The napalm of spring;
a tree all red at the tips, another
all yellow. We loosen our coats.
That time for three days along
the border on the Canadian side
girl-woman smiles drowned out Niagara
locking fingers: a turmeric cable car
across a bend in the green river
and further up a theatre street
in an English town or Asian?
Do not grow older by a second
do not let spears grow into leaves
and goodbyes and the rustling
of dresses; a friction of summer trees.

LITERARY TRANSLATIONS

Blue stars fluttering on tabletops
remind you it's windy and should be
spring. Winter creeps back like history;
girls wearing blue t-shirts, the Brookline
boys selling a holy land—not this land:
white triangulated six-pointed
blue on white is no stars and stripes.

The campus police arrives in black
near the big wall-flag with Arabic
characters (is there a script called
Palestinian?) We translate:
"kill the infidels"—the English says
"Victory to the Intifada."

The Israel club sells falafel
sweetened by dust and pollen
and the dried dung of
a pet loving metropolis. A nearby
tree is all pink blossoms.
We move away from the windows,
return to translating Psalms
and a German poet, Born's Berlin boys'
fascination with the Leatherstocking Saga.

THE BOARDING HOUSE (1)

Even an April rain of snow cannot tell you
how to bloom: pink blossoms hiding slender limbs
white flowers disguising a cabbage head of trees.
I do not know your name—an easy fix?
The volume of eastern flowering trees
gather dust until your touch; envelopes
neatly addressed hold old secrets and whispers
of a new world. I cannot tell you how to sing
through biscuit walls, as you fill your tub,
no more thinking we are too close. Neighbours
should not disturb each other. Strangers
should not sail into new lives. Columbus
was another time, or Marco Polo. I would,
of course, tell you of Vikramaditya but the phone
rings and you can hear my conversation. Every word,
if you care. In the cold, squirrels got under
the bonnet of the car. There were acorn shells
on the battery—a bed—and on the engine block.
The mechanic laughs as he drains the oil
and we clear the remnants of last year's nuts.
We can't tell squirrels where to roost in winter.

IN CENTRE COURT

One hundred faces and figures pass.
There is no time to see I's—
you hide behind a diamond-designed halfglass
behind unbagged book, take off your scarf.
Was that the same one you had in Toronto?
It is too hot inside April or the Laundromat
on Harvard Street. We didn't see when
you entered, busy placing soiled whites
in the washer, not quite red hair—a writing
professor saying, *say what it is, not what it isn't*—
cropped short and jagged like hibiscus plants
eaten hurriedly by goats, smile capping an almost
miniskirt when you sit and cross hairless legs,
and produce a novel, a smirk, and a pulling
down of hems. It can go no further, unless
we undo the clasp. You finger a green journal,
instead, undo the strap and scribble furiously,
no, I'm not a poet—just bringing things up-to-date.

We've read three books since, worked on a story,
read a dozen translations of a German poem
walked past a thousand blossoms of spring, yet
still recall those red knocked knees and almond eyes,
thin fingers clutching pen, violet ink unfurling
a net of lines triangulating the masts of Old Ironsides.

FRIDAY, APRIL 14

We try focusing on a great poet-translator's
Meditations on that famous Latin poet's,
"To a Tree on His Estate." Who toed your lower limb?
and didn't whisper, "Excuse me, may I pass?"
The room is warm today—the first time in months
and outside you were bubbling, six flights up.

It was a sagging tree and now you curse the planter,
the day—Horace, that is. Today is Good Friday.
We would have been singing a song: "Hot cross buns,
Hot cross buns." And the man from Nazareth
Would have been stumbling under eyes, more Roman
than Jew. Can I have a sip of water, a snip of bread?

The curry has been boiled in a foil package.
A new technology invented for the Indian Army.
We applaud fiercely after he says, "I'm eighty-two"
walks down six flights of stairs—alone—on a path
under leafless trees flushed with pink, white, purple:
cherry, plum, magnolias, showy ash,
green maple flowers (back in our room the boiled
curry, channa masala, grows cold). Further on,
the eastern white buds glowing all week, now carpet
the lawn and sidewalk like a shower
for newlyweds departing on honeymoon, are dead;
and we are saying goodbye to winter—and to spring.

ON THE BANKS OF THE CHARLES

Wrong age wrong place wrong time
for such volubility of blossoms—
spring exiting a mild winter.
I understand, finally, that parroting
of heart on your lips thin as ice
hot as a mirage six floors above
the Charles, sun glinting on the State House's
gold dome, sails and sailors tacking
in the wind on the water, heart
on the left-hand fingers' gesticulations
mind—wrong age wrong place wrong time
for dance on hearts on lips on fingers—
flaming forsythia ringing eastern redbud.

TRANSLATING HINDI POETRY IN SPRING

Tracking that forsythia on the thighs
of the Arnold Arboretum, we are coming
down into a bonsai garden distracted
by rhododendrons' flare of pink and Japanese
cherries transported to the hill.
These flowers don't bear fruit, won't,
like that other arboretum in Miami:
purple jamoons sweeter than the wines
of childhood; sapodilla, fruit of tropical
gods, honey-er than the skin of Penelope:
exile's attractiveness is returning; Rama
having slain Ravana takes a flying car . . .

And an aching heart on the southern bank
of a busy river among the fifth-floor shelves
reading yourself in a Caribbean anthology.
"I'm looking for Margaret Atwood," you said
squeezing by to the Canadian volumes. I met her
once. Dark eyes, dimpled smile, chin hairs
not shaved or plucked, but trimmed, gray
in the backlight. Flip-flops echoing places
lived: Ghana, Russia, Indian foothills
now controlled by terrorists: Hindi-purging?

Jackets off—I remember—you sing classical
Hindustani mixed with the world's rhythms
and why are you updating my flawed translations of
a deceased poet? This language we have yet to master
is all we share, all we are offering each other.

ODYSSEYS, MY LOVE

It was easier for Rama
Or Ulysses, whom you may know
Better—I too have kept faith
With Ithaca having never returned

In an hundred years or more. Hanuman—
Who? That one you may call
"the monkey God" was neither monkey
Nor man: my tail lit by a king's pride

Is torching a city, the yellow-red flames
Visible across the gulf. Why did we leave?
Or was that I, I, I—thin lipped men
Promising forests teeming with parakeets

Beyond the *Kala Pani*. Ulysses consorted
For seven years with swine loving women
Made music on calypso's bed. Still
I have not returned your touch falling

Like Taughannock's eyebrow-thin waterfall
For a continual mist. We are a dream.
Rama returned after fourteen years
And you will now understand that question:

What is our Ithaca, where our Ayodhya?
Georgetown, where red samans fall
on Main Street, and cassia-golden rods
rival the midday sun, and sugarcane

swaying to the dholak of coconut palms,
where the sweeter-than-honey sapodillas
ripen and fall on an evening
bed of waiting toast leaves?

I have kept faith, I tell you—Ulysses'
Nothing and Rama's knowing Hanuman's
Chest, when opened to Sita, is a flower
Still scented and waiting your touch.

OVID IN EXILE

The golden dome of State House
sparkles in the vapored sunshine
and an April fog creeps up,
crosses the Harvard Bridge's arches
in the instep of your feet.

You do not feel cold sitting,
looking out, following
the meshed shoe's tilt away
from heels. Hillbillies don't come
from New York, upstate
somewhere in the Appalachians.

You had "noone" instead of "noon."
A small thing. Why didn't I shut up?
Luckily, distance is not the fertilizer
of anger—no?—the rocks we prized
out of the unpaved street are still

dusty on my fingers: I aim at
a dead dog in the canal, thud!
move along with your flies: words
and poet-mongers. I will not hear
your voice again, or feel your feet lock
my calf. Do not make love over

this distance of eyes. And I did
shut up, when I should have said,
come, let us have tea, come spend
that night after we ungown.
If I can't come home
can't you come from home

with sapodilla-soursop-seed eyes,
freshly squeezed cane-juice
lips. There is a shadow in the land
(you use prepositions strangely)
of legs. A dark soil of pudendum

when the waves burst on the old Dutch
seawall: a salt spray you never taste again.
You are gone, the coconut fronds
fingers of your left hand shaking the fruited air.
After all this time, you never did take me
home, or "bring" me from my exiled bed.

DO NOT SAY GOODBYE

Lemon-green buds cover the tarmac.
Young maple leaves laugh
in the wind. This is not the way
to say goodbye; not in the pub
by a cold river, or a coffee house
cozy and comforted by a dozen ears
listening for tomorrow. Do not look back
to this piped time; the one who talked
too much, the one whose ears went out
to space, whose hair fell like a flaxen
Kaiteur; I've been there, I know
it all, Manhattan's the world . . . Or
another head framed by the Charles,
Concord grape eyes; we didn't make
that reading. Pretend, at least, we're friends
happy for each other; we will
keep in touch, some separately; we will
become famous; I know no irony—I do
not know "American," or own a dictionary,
in Georgetown English—eh!—South America
we cuss you to your face. We take everything
personally—even blossoms falling
on your hair. How flows the Demerara,
dear brother, still out to the Atlantic?
Do not say goodbye, until we're gone.

SCULPTOR

Hair molded in a pony.
We didn't see your fingers—
eyes as silky as the magnets
we touched once, twice joining
two bodies of cement
smooth, not smoother
than a sculptor's skin.
Such fingers, hand, strength, warmth—
I never entered Vermont, green plates
all I know, you never the Vineyard.

This must be that space between
Cape Cod and the green mountains
we knew. Dedham Rock, gray concrete
we touch again, in puja, exiting.
We will never meet again, we can tell
not for the first time, words are useless.

What will last longer than stone?
Skin, you think. Heart, you think
soul of a sculptor's fingers.

TOMORROW I WILL WALK DOWN TO BOSTON HARBOUR

(For "Sash", late Minister of Agriculture, assassinated along with his brother, sister, and guard)

You did not have to return
and, yes you did driving
through unpretty snowstorms
a spring picnic of exiles
in the Morningside Park
chilly, even for apple
blossoms and the dead-white
skins of peeling paper birches

take a shot of XM or
Eldorado rum for the cold
fingers, dalpuri to warm
stomachs. In Danny's car
on highway 7, or another
time in the bus returning
from Ottawa—I have pictures
in black and white: picketing

on Parliament Hill near
the eternal flame, meeting
a minor government official,
please help restore democracy
to our land. Forget it all.
We're in the chartered bus
travelling back to Toronto,

meadows of red flowers, fields
of yellow daisies flashing past.
I could gather some, now,
here in the greening fields

of Boston; this highest hill
looking over, in the distance,
a balcony on which colonists
read The Declaration, went
to that famous party dressed
as natives. You would have loved

such a prank. Bunker Hill wasn't.
"The whites of their eyes"
must have been visible—not the
shot from behind. You did
have to go back to that land
ashes, now, all remaining
of all we knew; I will break
every rule of grammar and
"good writing," Mr Editor,
but I shall never set foot

on that soil again
as you have: many homes and
none. Tomorrow I will walk
down to Boston harbour
and spill tea in your memory.

PROVIDENCE

Kicked out from Plymouth
Roger Williams lived
with the Wampanog.
Who were these enemies
of the Puritans in whose
cabins he hid that winter?

Perhaps, it was a weekend
in May, when the Narragansett
gave him land. Whom?
The guidebook doesn't say.

Come up the hill, you said,
Halfway and turn left.

In the restaurant, I try Italian
cheese. Husband a reluctant host
until we get to Virgil.
That was a long time back.
The best poetry survives:
Will everyone cite Shakespeare?

Talking about the Georgics,
an agricultural manual that is not
on planting or reaping or sowing—
you must not write unfocused poetry.
A good spouse walks up the hill,
returning to a dissertation on the classics.

We walk down to a craft show.
The story of the white dogwoods,
I hear for the first time, represents
Christ on the cross. You never think

about the wood they used—toes
in tight sandals need adjusting—
what is wrong with this sentence:
The first Baptist church is closed.

We could join a walking tour
for a fee, or visit used bookstores,
a coffee shop sharing chocolate
cake, the lot next door cleared
and ready for builders; an infant
tugging his mother's leg stops
and looks at our faces through the glass.
In Texas, people still fly
Confederate flags attached
to the backs of trucks—in Florida too.

We are talking about you
who will not talk to me. If
we could talk longer over coffee,
tour the city, admire a gondola
in the canal. Down the river, boats
came laden with slaves and sugar
from the West Indies. We merge
days, periods. Walking up the hill,

up somewhere, we had smelled wisteria
I could see the next day on BU buildings—
we are stopping and smelling lilacs
today on the arboretum's lilac path
the scent of a son running across
a month-of-Toronto fields, picking up
sticks; a fresh-cut bunch perfuming
the apartment. We might have slept
outside that night—I can't recall

what I saw with every step
were toes—soul residing in feet
takes our hearts to distant places
in a supermarket shopping for bread,
riding a mustang down centuries—
where was Williams born?

No matter. It was what he did,
giving thanks, having passed through
a strange winter; calling this space
we share, following your bare toes, Providence.

HOUSE ON THE HILL

If I walked up Summit Hill again,
stopped in front your green house
listening to the soul of your home:
how the radiator wall is un-insulated
how the hedge was too high,
blocking the light, so you upended them
how we couldn't figure the blossoming
tree's name, pink petals strewn on the ground
in the rain, worried of the roots
interfering with gas line and water line—
if I walked on your red-brick footpath,
rang your bell under the light
you've left on, we could never meet again
as we did yesterday in your gloved hand in
the folds of your frockcoat and gulf-green eyes.

BOSTON, YOU IS A BITCH

After those sun-blotted weeks
of ashed trunks loitering
everywhere horned crowns
etching those temperamental
indigo eyes overhead

After those long months
of cavernous brownstones
and redstones on the hill,
an address on Beacon Street

After the interminable rains
in that record breaking month
flooded basements and cancelled
outdoor gatherings, you opened
your sandscaled redstone legs.

Copley Square was filled.
Shoppers generated traffic jams.
The hunt for parking
favored smaller cars.
White petals fluttering

Or red in this part of town
yellow forsythia like cusps
of pubic hair and Harbans
muttering and mouthing louder
with a Bengal-tiger's smile,

"Boston, you is a Bitch. A bitch
I tell you! But I will return."

THE BOARDING HOUSE (2)

Touching the harmonium's black
keys, singing a dhun and stopping
a Florida night in a Boston's
I couldn't make out your melody
was sweeter than any Demerara
sugar. The closest we came
to conversation: Are you off
on holiday then? No. I'm finished.
So quickly? Yes. Goodbye? Yes.
You toss that cabbage
head into your room. I do not know
your name. I will forget these brown
walls, snow boots outside your door
uncaredfor shoes. We crossed in the rain
barely recognizing each other's umbrellas.
I will never know you again.
If we pass, it will be as strangers.

ACKNOWLEDGEMENTS

Acknowledgements are due to: Sharief Khan and the *Guyana Chronicle* in which, "Tomorrow I will Walk down to Boston Harbour" appeared in a slightly different form; to Peter Nazareth and Kirpal Singh for publishing "Odysseys, My Love" in *Interlogue: Studies in Singapore Literature Volume 7: Edwin Thumboo;* to Boston University and to Leslie Epstein for the Leslie Epstein Fellowship; to all the people in Boston and New England who touched and enriched my life: Matt Yost; Laurence Breiner; Aaron Fogel; Jennifer Haigh; Xuefie (Ha) Jin; William Waters and a gathering of engaging translators; Jennifer Hunt; the 236 group—Andrew, Brett, David, Emma, Joe, Lauren K, Lauren T, Melissa, Ted, and Mary; Deborah Nestor, Sunil Sharma, Tonetta, Chris and Marilyn Pauli; all the people I did not mention due entirely to a mind which is more partial to remembering faces and acts of generosity than names; Peter Nazareth, ever willing to read and suggest changes; my publisher at TSAR, Nurjehan, for her patience and generosity; my relatives and family: Dian and Michael, Prem, JuneAnne; Sharon, Tekil, and Kshanika, all of whom helped make this book a reality.